Scuba Diving

by Michael Teitelbaum

Published by The Child's World®
1980 Lookout Drive
Mankato, MN 56003-1705
800-599-READ
www.childsworld.com

The Child's World®: Mary Berendes, Publishing Director
Shoreline Publishing Group, LLC: James Buckley Jr.,
 Production Director
The Design Lab: Design and production

ISBN: 978-1-60973-182-3
LCCN: 2011928872

Photo credits: Cover: Dreamstime.com/Richard Carey.
Interior: Ralph Clevenger: 20, 23, 28; Corbis: 7, 8;
dreamstime.com: Deborah Coles 4, Richard Carey 11,
Jimmy Lopes 12, Serghei Starus 15, Jonmilnes 19,
Rebecca Picard 24, Debra James 27; iStock: 16.

Printed in the United States of America
Mankato, Minnesota
July, 2011
PA02094

Table of Contents

Scuba diving makes it possible to explore the undersea world.

CHAPTER ONE

Under the Sea

Imagine yourself exploring a sunken pirate ship filled with ancient treasure. You glide from room to room, swimming beside fish, searching for a treasure chest or a sack of gold **doubloons**. Are you dreaming? No, you are scuba diving!

Scuba diving is a way for people to breathe underwater. It allows us to see amazing things and beautiful animals we would not be able to see any other way.

Scuba is actually an **acronym**. Its letters stand for Self Contained Underwater Breathing Apparatus. This system of diving was invented in 1943 by Jacques Cousteau, a French scientist who studied the ocean and life under the sea.

People have been trying to invent ways to breathe underwater for thousands of years. In the 1500s, people went into the ocean in wooden barrels with only one or two breaths of air trapped inside. In the 1700s, the air pump was invented. This allowed air from the surface to be pumped to divers below. This was first used to pump air into wooden barrels to allow those divers to stay underwater longer.

The long hose sent air down to the diver after he **submerged**.

Jacques Cousteau's invention opened up the undersea world to exploration.

By the 1800s, people used diving suits with large metal helmets. A long air hose attached to the helmet pumped air to the diver. However, the hose meant that the diver couldn't move very fast or very far.

Scuba diving changed all that. With scuba gear, divers carry the air supply with them. No more long hoses are needed. The diver can go anyplace . . . or at least until the air in his tank runs out!

Today people dive for all kinds of reasons. They dive for **recreation**, exploration, and scientific study. They dive to search for lost ships and missing treasure. Some people dive for fun, some dive to earn a living. All of them get to view a world most people never see—the world under the sea.

Jacques Cousteau
Frenchman Jacques Cousteau was a man of the sea. A former French naval officer, he later spent a lot of time warning of the dangers of pollution. He was a photographer, filmmaker, and author. Many people saw him as host of a long-running television series—*The Undersea World of Jacques Cousteau*. He and Emile Gagnan invented scuba in 1943. Their invention was first put to use by divers to remove enemy mines at the end of World War II.

CHAPTER TWO

Take Your Air With You

Fish have no problem breathing underwater. They have **gills**, a special body part that allows them to take oxygen out of the water. Unfortunately, humans don't have gills. If we want to breathe underwater, we need to bring our oxygen with us. That's where scuba diving gear comes in.

The oxygen is stored in a metal tank that is strapped to a scuba diver's back. Early scuba divers learned quickly there's more to diving than just having air. The deeper a diver goes, the more pressure builds up on his or her chest and lungs. This makes it difficult to breathe underwater.

The fish has gills . . .
the scuba diver has to
bring her air with her.

The diver holds the regulator firmly in his mouth. The mask lets him see clearly.

To fix this problem, modern scuba gear includes a **regulator** (REG-yoo-lay-tor). The regulator is attached to a mouthpiece. It makes sure that the air the diver breathes is at exactly the right pressure.
On land, most people breathe through their noses. But scuba divers usually breathe through their mouths.

Because it is difficult to see clearly underwater, scuba divers also wear masks. A piece of specially made glass is held in a rubber or plastic frame. A tight strap holds the mask to the face and keeps water from entering.

In order to sink into the water, scuba divers need to wear special jackets. The jackets are called **Buoyancy** Control Devices (BCD). These jackets are filled with weights that help divers sink. They also help divers float easily once they have reached whatever depth they want.

The deep parts of the ocean are very, very cold. Fish have skin that can handle the cold, but people don't. That's why scuba divers need to wear wet suits. Wet suits are made from a special material called neoprene (NEE-oh-preen). They fit tightly, like a second skin, covering the whole body. Wet suits keep scuba divers warm.

Divers need a lot of gear to be safe underwater.

15

Fins, also called flippers, are long, flat pieces of rubber or plastic that attach to a diver's feet. These imitate the fins that fish have. When the scuba diver kicks his or her legs, the fins wave up and down. This motion pushes the diver through the water.

Swimmers keep track of how much air they have left with a special dial. They can also take a device that tells them how deep they are. A compass can come in handy to tell direction. There are no road signs in the ocean!

These divers kick with fins to move. They're also being pulled by motorized mini-sleds.

Finally, the most important thing to bring when diving is a buddy. Even the most expert divers know to never dive alone. Divers working together keep an eye on each other and can get help in case of trouble.

Scuba diving is very safe, but only if divers are careful and use the buddy system.

Along with safety, dive buddies help each other discover sea life such as this octopus.

Most fishermen stay above the water, but diving
helps this man search for lobsters.

CHAPTER THREE

Explore the Unknown

Most people dive for fun, but for some people, diving is a job. Scientists, of course, dive to study fish and the sea itself. Some divers work for oil companies trying to find new sources of oil under the ocean floor. Others work as welders, repairing underwater gear that can only be reached by divers. Other scuba-diving workers install underwater pipelines for oil, gas, fresh water, or electricity along the ocean's floor.

Divers inspect and repair boats. Others help **salvage** ships that have sunk to the bottom of the ocean. This is called wreck diving. Underwater photographers take photos and video for magazines, TV shows, or movies.

Scuba divers are an important part of the military, too. Military divers, known as "frogmen," sometimes engage in underwater combat. Frogmen can also slip behind enemy lines without being spotted. They can place underwater mines or spy on enemy ships.

Underwater photographers use special cameras to capture undersea scenes.

The darker blue water is the Great Blue Hole off the coast of Belize.

Police divers search for clues in lakes or oceans. Along with fire department divers, they perform search and recovery or rescue operations for those in trouble underwater.

But where do these divers do their diving? There are lots of great places around the world.

Jacques Cousteau called the Great Blue Hole in Belize one of the best dive spots in the world. The water is crystal-clear and home to a huge amount of sea life. Divers can go down as much as 400 feet (122 m).

Sipadan, in Malaysia, is also a top dive site. Divers swim with turtles, sharks, dolphins, and brilliantly colored schools of fish. These creatures live on a colorful coral reef. Sipadan also has a system of connected caves for divers to explore.

Perhaps the most famous and spectacular dive site in the world is the Great Barrier Reef in Australia. This super-sized reef is actually made up of almost 3,000 individual reefs, stretching along 900 islands for a distance of 1,600 miles (2,475 km). It is filled with colorful fish and beautiful coral.

Australia's Great Barrier Reef gets divers
up close to amazing sea life.

If you become a diver, who knows?
Maybe you can dance with sea lions.

Scuba diving is a great way to see amazing sites. Many people combine scuba diving with other travel. They make trips to explore sights on land as well as take diving trips offshore. Scuba diving helps scientists examine the mysterious world beneath the ocean's surface. For some people, scuba diving is the way they make a living.

No matter why they dive, with scuba gear, human beings can swim with the fish and other undersea wonders.

Glossary

acronym—an abbreviation made up of the first letter of each word in a phrase

buoyancy—the ability to float in water

doubloons—ancient gold coins

gills—part of a fish that allows them remove and breathe the oxygen in water

recreation—the process of having fun or doing an activity that is not work-related

regulator—a scuba diving device that controls the air a diver breathes

salvage—anything recovered from being lost or thrown away

submerged—sunk beneath water or other liquid

BOOKS

Scuba Diving
By Carol Ryback. Milwaukee, WI: Gareth Stevens, 2005.
An introduction to the world of scuba diving, with colorful photos.

Scuba Diving, Active Sports
By Valerie Bodden. Mankato, MN: Creative Education, 2009.
An oversized book about the sport, with information and color photos.

Scuba Diving, Living on the Edge
By Shane McFee. New York, NY: PowerKids Press, 2008.
A look at the exciting (and extreme!) sport of scuba diving.

WEB SITES

For links to learn more about extreme sports: **childsworld.com/links**

Note to Parents, Teachers, and Librarians: We routinely verify our Web links to make sure they are safe and active sites. So encourage your readers to check them out!

Index

About the Author

Michael Teitelbaum has been a writer and editor of children's books and magazines for more than twenty years. Michael's most recent nonfiction includes *Jackie Robinson: Champion For Equality*, published by Sterling. His fiction includes *The Scary States of America* and books based on characters ranging from Spider-Man and Batman to Garfield and Kermit the Frog.